The Manifesto of the Logocratic Party

The Manifesto of the Logocratic Party

Daniel Deleanu

iUniverse, Inc.
New York Lincoln Shanghai

The Manifesto of the Logocratic Party

iUniverse, Inc.

For information address:
iUniverse, Inc.
2021 Pine Lake Road, Suite 100
Lincoln, NE 68512
www.iuniverse.com

ISBN: 0-595-33589-6

Printed in the United States of America

To my dear wife, Codrutza

Motto: "Follow your Word!"

—Daniel Deleanu

Contents

The Manifesto of the Logocratic Party

The world is undergoing a profound change. Humanity, uneasy in this computer age, is demanding a sense of security and dignity based on human values.

Not a single government which fails to recognize this trend—and take appropriate action—can survive.

That is why the Logocratic Party has moved to keep ahead of this trend; has moved with speed incomprehensible to those who do not see this trend.

Today, established institutions are being overthrown and demagogical democratic philosophies are being installed by those whose creed recognizes no power higher than military force, no values other than a false efficiency and material gain. Martin Luther King was right when he said that "We are prone to judge success by the index of our salaries or the size of our automobile rather than by the quality of our service and relationship to mankind."

What the founding fathers of democracy realized was a daring dream, that human beings could have not only physical security, not only efficiency, but something else in addition that humans had never had before—the security of the heart that comes with freedom, the peace of mind that comes from a sense of justice. Unfortunately, this remained a dream.

To this generation of people who live in the digital era, it is given to turn this dream of liberty into reality. The world maladjustment against which we prepare our defense is so threatening that not until it has burned itself out in the last corner of the earth will our faith be able to relax its guard. And that is because we "have come to the conclusion that politics is too serious a matter to be left to the politicians" (Charles De Gaulle).

The term "democracy" comes from the Greek words *demos*, meaning "people," and *kratos*, signifying "power." The actual meaning of democracy is that the power lies in the hands of the people, that is *human beings*. Logocracy, on the other hand, is a coinage of the Greek words *Logos* ("Reason," "Divine Word," "Willing Principle") and *kratos* ("power"). Thus, logocracy is a political system in which the power is attributed to God and Reason. *Logocracy is not a theocracy*, that means a form of government in which the governmental rulers are identical with the leaders of the dominant religion.

Logocracy is the daughter of the interdisciplinary philosophical system called *logosophism* (see our book *Principles of Logosophism*). Logocracy is a political doctrine destined for believers (Logos = Divine Word), as well as for non-believers (Logos = Reason). We believe that the Logos is the main archetype of humanity (see our book *The Logoarchetype*), since the Word is associated with the Divinity in almost all the religions of the world. Logocracy believes in the power of the Word seen as the Divine (Logos), and in the power of the word conceived as reason (logos).

These days, every one seems to have forgotten Abraham Lincoln's wise words: "Quarrel not at all. No man resolved to make the most of himself can spare time for personal contention. Still less can he afford to take all the consequences, including the vitiating of his temper and loss of self-control." Yet, today, politics equates with fighting; politics does not mean civilized, polite debating anymore, but rather a neverending argument. It does not matter anymore what one politician proposes in the legislature. If he or she belongs to the opposition, his or her words are always injustly and impolitely rejected, without being given the slightest consideration. The parliament, once an agora where valuable political ideas used to be exchanged in a polite and fruitful fashion, has become a circus of clowns. With a few notable exceptions, to be a politician today is the synonym of being a liar or even a thief. "Every election is a sort of advance auction sale of stolen goods" states H. L. Mencken, while Ronald Reagan sarcastically tells us: "politics is supposed to be the second-oldest profession, but I have come to realize that it bears a very close resemblance to the first". Gore Vidal does not display more optimism about the quality of today's political class when he complains that "Today's public figures can no longer write their own speeches or books, and there is some evidence that they can't read them either."

Logocracy wants to reestablish the lost dignity of the politician. Logocracy promotes a policy of truth ("The search for truth is more precious than its possession" has said Albert Einstein). That is why the supporters of the Logocratic Party lo not wish to register the Party in any country of the world. By registering the Party in one or more countries of the world, the supporters of the Party would become members, and finally "professional" politicians, pursuing personal goals and eventually being no better than the rest of the world's political class. That is why the Logocratic Party has no official members, only supporters and enthusiasts. This is the proof of the honesty of the policies promoted by the Logocratic Party: "Superior leaders get things done with very little motion. They impart instruction not through many words, but through a few deeds. They keep informed about everything but interfere hardly at all. They are catalysts, and though things would not get done as well if they were not there, when they succeed they take no credit. And, because they take no credit, credit never leaves them" (Lao Tzu).

The supporters of the Logocratic Party shall not be elected in any parliament of the world; they shall, on the other way, strive to educate and inspire, challenge and change. This will, beyond any shadow of a doubt, *make a difference.* Mahatma Gandhi has clearly advised: "Be the change you want to see in the world. First they ignore you, then they laugh at you, then they fight you, then you win."

The Logocratic Party favours politics in contrast to politicianism.

The Logocratic Party does not have a constitution, since it does not believe in constitutions. The Romanian scholar and politician Nicolae Iorga-one of the greatest spirits who have ever walked on this earth (he has penned 1359 books and over 25,000 articles!)-clearly stated in 1925: "I do not believe in magical constitutions, but in the consciousness which spontaneously promulgates constitutional articles, even though they have never been put down on paper."

In this world crisis, the purpose of the Logocratic Party is to defend against external attack and justify by internal progress the systems of government around the world from which the Logocratic Party takes its name. It is our duty to revolutionize the fossilized and futile concept of democracy, as we know it today, in a global environment of political corruption. It is our duty to show the world once again the road to honour and good sense. But, as Confucius has said, "to put the world right in order, we must first put the nation in order; to put the nation in order, we must first put the family in order; to put the family in order, we must first cultivate our personal life; we must first set our hearts right." And Socrates has solemnly declared: "Let him who would move the world first move himself," while Winston Churchill once said, "Never give in—never, never, never, never, in nothing great or small, large or petty, never give in except to convictions of honour and good sense."

Towards the modern fulfillment of the libertarian ideal, the Logocratic Party, during the last few years, has laboured successfully:

1. To strengthen human rights by defensive preparedness against political corruption, whether by open attack or secret infiltration;

2. To strengthen personal freedom by increasing economic efficiency (there cannot be real freedom without the minimum of material comfort); and

3. To strengthen civil liberties by improving the welfare of the world nations through the implementation of a logocratic economy.

These three objectives are one and inseparable. No nation can be strong by armaments alone. It must possess and use all the necessary resources for producing goods plentifully and distributing them effectively. It must add to these factors of material strength the unconquerable spirit and energy of a contented planetary nation, convinced that there are no boundaries to human progress and happiness in, as Marshall McLuhan has named it, our "global village", which should become a realm of peace and liberty.

Our faith that these objectives can be attained is made unshakable by what has already been done by the great political figures of the world, without any partisanship or prejudicial configuration—in stopping the waste and exploitation of our human and natural resources, in restoring to the average man and woman a stake in the preservation of our civil liberties, in consolidating our national identities, and in achieving international unity in our big *multicultural village* by the name of Planet Earth.

We shall hold fast to these gains. We are proud of our record. Therefore, the Logocratic Party endorses wholeheartedly the brilliant and courageous leadership and platforms of such great figures as Socrates, Plato, Aristotle, Confucius, Lao Tzu, St. Thomas Aquinas, Jean-Jacques Rousseau, George Washington, Abraham Lincoln, Karl Marx, Ralph Waldo Emerson, Leo Tolstoy, Winston Churchill, Albert Einstein, Martin Luther King and Nelson Mandela. And to our great source of inspiration and leader, Mahatma Gandhi, we send him, wherever he is, our cordial greetings and our humble obeisance.

The Logocratic Party sustains neither the capitalist system nor the communist one; at the same time, the Logocratic Party can be seen as a synthesis of both. Yet, the Logocratic Party does not believe in any political "-ism". Humanity has experienced both capitalism and communism, and has realized that both have their flaws. We should learn from our own mistakes, and at the same time we should take what is good from both systems ("Black cat or white cat makes no difference as long as it catches the mice" said Deng Xiao-Ping). The theories of both Adam Smith and Karl Marx have their highs and lows. Both in James Stuart Mill, David Ricardo and Ayn Rand, on the one hand, and in Vladimir Ilych Lenin, Mao Tse-Tung and Che Guevara, on the other, one can find valuable ideas. As for those who have sinned on the political scene, remember Mahatma Gandhi's words of wisdom: "Hate the sin and love the sinner."

Of course, we are not naïve: we know that this political credo will have to face a lot of harsh criticism from both sides ("Standing in the middle of the road is very dangerous; you may get knocked down by traffic from both sides"—Margaret Thatcher). Yet, we courageously assume this risk.

The emerging logocratic nations will not participate in foreign wars, and will not send armies, naval or air forces to fight in foreign lands, except in case of attack. We favour and shall rigorously enforce and defend Mahatma Gandhi's doctrine of *satyagraha* (non-violence and non-cooperation in any enterprise that leads or might lead to war).

The direction and aim of any foreign policy in a logocratic state will be the maintenance of world peace.

At this hour, organized assaults against religion, egalitarianism, equity and international good faith are threatening our own peace and security. Corrupt politicians blinded by partisanship are brushing aside these warnings as officious intermeddling. The fall of nations was necessary to bring their belated approval of legislative and executive action that the United Nations had urged and undertaken with the full support of many of the world's nations. It is a tribute to the Logocratic Party's foresight and action that our defense forces are today at the peak of their peacetime effectiveness. Yet, military preparation should not be belligerent in its core, but rather pacifying.

We have seen the downfall of nations accomplished through internal dissension provoked from without. We denounce and will do all in our power to destroy the treasonable activities of disguised anti-libertarian agencies which would sap our strength, paralyze our will to defend ourselves, and destroy our unity by inciting race against race, class against class, religion against religion and the people against their free institutions.

To make world nations strong, and to keep them free, every inhabitant of the "global village" must give of their talents and treasure in accordance with their ability and their country's needs. For this, we must possess the spirit of sacrifice as well as the spirit of opportunity, and in order to acquire them, we must also have a lot of wisdom: that is because, as V. I. Lenin has put it, "it is far more difficult to unearth a dozen wise men than a hundred fools."

To insure that our armaments shall be implements of peace rather than war, we shall promote our traditional policies of the good neighbour; observe and advocate international respect for the fights of others and for treaty obligations; cultivate foreign trade through desirable trade agreements; and foster economic collaboration among all the countries of the world.

In a spirit of so-called "self-defense" and "good conscience", the so-called "world's greatest democracies" can afford heartlessly or in a spirit of appeasement to ignore the peace-loving and liberty-loving peoples wantonly attacked by ruthless aggressors. We pledge not to extend to these people any spiritual or material aid that is inconsistent with the international laws and the provisions of the United Nations—all to the end that peace and international good faith may yet emerge triumphant.

We do not regard the need for preparedness a warrant for infringement upon our civil liberties; but, on the contrary, we shall continue to protect them, in the keen realization that the vivid contrast between the freedom we enjoy and the dark repression, which prevails in the lands where democracy has killed our civil liberties, affords warning and example to our people to confirm their faith in logocracy ("Our duty is to hold ourselves responsible to the other people. Every word, every act and every policy must confirm to the people's interests, and if mistakes occur, they must be corrected-that is what being responsible to the people means"—Mao Tse-Tung).

The well-being of the land and those who work upon it is basic to the real defense and security of the world's nations.

The Logocratic Party gives its promises to the farmers and its allegiance to those who exploit them.

We pledge ourselves:

To make parity as well as soil conservation payments until such time as the goal of parity income for agriculture is realized.

To extend and enlarge the machinery-purchase program until every deserving tenant farmer has a real opportunity to have a firm of his or her own.

To refinance existing farm debts at lower interest rates and on longer and more flexible terms.

To continue to provide for adjustment of production through logocratic processes to the extent that excess surpluses are capable of control.

To continue the program of rehabilitation of farmers who need and merit aid.

To preserve and strengthen national granaries which should contribute to the creation of an international granary, meant to help in the eradication of starvation in the majority of the underdeveloped countries.

To continue to make commodity loans to maintain the ever-normal granary and to prevent destructively low or high prices.

To send all national surpluses to the developing countries, thus bringing surplus farm commodities to needy consumers.

To increase all the necessary appropriations for research and extension work through the land-grant colleges, and for research laboratories established to develop new outlets for farm products.

To conserve the soil and water resources for the benefit of farmers and nations they represent. In such conservation programs we shall, so far as practicable, bring about that development in forests and other permanent crops as will not unduly expand livestock and dairy production.

To safeguard the farmers' foreign markets and expand their domestic and international markets for all domestic and international crops, as established by the basic principles of a logocratic economy.

To encourage the logocratic development of the world's river basins through reclamation and irrigation, flood control, reforestation and soil conservation, stream purification, recreation, fish and game protection, low-cost power, and rural industry, in the spirit of a viable ecological program, as that expounded, for example, by Green Peace.

To encourage marketing agreements in aid of producers of dairy products, vegetables, fruits and specialty crops for the purpose of orderly marketing and the avoidance of unfair and wasteful practices.

To extend crop insurance from wheat to other crops as rapidly as experience justifies such extension.

To safeguard both big farms and family-sized farms in all our logocratic programs, whether they are private or government-owned.

To finance these programs adequately in order that they may be effective.

In settling new lands reclaimed from desert by scientific projects, we shall give priority to homeless families who have lost their farms. As these new lands are brought into use, we shall continue by governmental purchase to retire from the plow submarginal lands so that an increased percentage of the world's farmers may he able to live and work on good land.

These logocratic programs will continue to be in the hands of locally-elected farmer committees to the largest extent possible. In this truly logocratic way, we will continue to bring economic security to the farmer and his or her family, while recognizing the dignity and freedom of farm life in all the countries of the world. Adam Smith has highlighted in *The Wealth of Nations*:

> The produce of almost all other labour is liable to the like deduction of profit. In all arts and manufactures the greater part of the workmen stand in need of a master to advance them the materials of their work, and their wages and maintenance till it be completed. He shares in the produce of their labour, or in the value which it adds to the materials upon which it is bestowed; and in this share consists his profit. It sometimes happens, indeed, that a single independent workman has stock sufficient both to purchase the materials of his work, and to maintain himself till it be completed. He is both master and workman, and enjoys the whole produce of his own labour, or the whole value which it adds to the materials upon which it is bestowed. It includes what are

usually two distinct revenues, belonging to two distinct persons, the profits of stock, and the wages of labour.

Under the so-called "democratic auspices," little has been done in the last fifty years to foster the essential freedom, dignity and opportunity of the world's workers. In consequence, labour today cannot take its rightful place as a partner of management in the common cause of higher earnings, industrial efficiency, and national and international unity.

A far-flung system of international corporate maneuvers has brought together millions and millions of confused workers and a great deal of unemployment. The workers' right to organize and bargain collectively through representatives of their own choosing should be encouraged in all the countries of the world. We should enlarge the international machinery for the mediation of labour disputes. We should enact an effective wage and hour law. Child labour in factories has been outlawed, but it still exists in so many countries, including the so-called democratic ones. Sweat-shops ruin the integrity of so many workers, but at the same time they are the only way these people can make a living. These are the big issues the Logocratic Party plans to have in view.

We pledge to continue to enforce fair labour standards; to create a set of principles materialized in an International Labour Relations Act; to expand employment training and opportunity for our youth, older workers, and workers displaced by technological changes; to strengthen the orderly processes of collective bargaining and peaceful settlement of labour disputes; and to work always for a just distribution of the national income among those who labour. As Karl Marx stated in *The Communist Manifesto*:

> The average price of wage labour is the minimum wage, i.e., that quantum of the means of subsistence which is absolutely requisite to keep the labourer in bare existence as a labourer. What, therefore, the wage labourer appropriates by means of his labour merely suffices to prolong and reproduce a bare existence. We by no means intend to abolish this personal appropriation of the products of labour, an appropriation that is made for the maintenance and reproduction of human life, and that leaves no surplus wherewith to command the labour of others. All that we want to do away with is the miserable character of this appropriation, under which the labourer lives merely to increase capital...

We shall continue our efforts to promote equality of opportunity for men and women without impairing the social legislation which promotes true equality by safeguarding the health, safety and economic welfare of workers. The right to work for compensation in both public and private employment is an inalienable privilege of women as well as men, without distinction as to marital status.

The production of oil is one of our most important basic industries. Stability of production, employment, distribution and price are indispensable to the public welfare. We pledge sympathetic consideration of the revision of the OPEC policies to the oil industry, in order to provide additional protection for the owners, miners and consumers of oil and crude products.

We shall continue to emphasize the human element in industry and strive toward increasingly wholehearted cooperation between labour and industrial management.

To make logocracy strong, the system of business enterprise, both private and public, must be free to gear its tremendous productive capacity to serve the greatest good of the greatest number, without taking into the consideration whether the initiative is private or public. Mahatma Gandhi has declared: "The things that will destroy us are: politics without principle; pleasure without conscience; wealth without work; knowledge without character; business without morality; science without humanity; and worship without sacrifice."

We shall defend all legitimate business, but shall strongly oppose any corrupt or illegal form of business activity.

We have attacked and will continue to attack unbridled concentration of economic power and the exploitation of the consumer and the investor.

We shall oppose the kind of banking which treats developing countries as financial colonies; the kind of securities business which regard the stock exchange as a private gambling club for wagering other people's money; the kind of public utility holding companies which used consumers' and investors' money to suborn a free press, bludgeon legislatures and political conventions, and control elections against the interest of their customers and their security holders.

We shall strongly oppose the kind of business which levies tribute on all the rest of the world free market by the extortionate methods of monopoly.

We do not stop with criticism and opposition—we follow through with the remedy. People will find in themselves, through the logocratic process, ability to meet the economic problems of the average business where concentrated power has failed.

We nowadays have a broken and prostrate banking and financial system all around the world. We shall restore it to health by strengthening banks, insurance companies and other financial institutions. We promote the protection of millions and millions of small investors, private and public, in the security and commodity markets. We shall thus revive confidence, safeguarded thrift, and open the road to all honourable business, both private and public.

We propose that the much-promised crediting at low interest rates be made available to small-business owners as soon as possible by such international financial institutions such as the World Bank, thus unfastening the oppressive yoke of a money monopoly, and giving the ordinary citizen a chance to go into business and stay in business.

We recognize the importance of small business concerns and new enterprises in our national economies, and favour the enactment of constructive national and international legislations to safeguard the welfare of small business, both private and public. Public large-scale enterprise, no less than private business, should be adequately represented on appropriate governmental boards and commissions, and its interests should be examined and fostered by a continuous research program.

The logocratic economy should provide an important outlet for both private and public capital by stimulating home building and low-rent housing projects.

The Logocratic Party should foster a well-balanced logocratic merchant marine and the world's finest system of civil aeronautics, to promote logocratic commerce and international defense.

The Logocratic Party, through the creation of a logocratic economy, should steer a steady course between a bankruptcy-producing deflation and a thrift-destroying inflation.

We shall continue to oppose barriers which impede trade among the countries of the world. We pledge our best efforts in strengthening all the national markets, and to this end we favour the adjustment of freight rates so that no country will have undue advantage over any other.

To encourage investment in "unproductive" enterprise (culture, education, some sports, etc.), the tax-exempt privileges should be maintained and encouraged.

We should enforce the anti-trust laws more vigorously than at any time in our history, thus affording the maximum protection to the competitive system.

We favour strict supervision of all forms of the insurance business by the national governments for the protection of policy holders and the public.

We support not only the elevation of the quantity level of consumer demand, which is supposed to quicken the flow of buying and selling through every artery of industry and trade, but also the increase of the quality of consumer demand. The Logocratic Party favours consume in contrast to consumerism.

With mass purchasing power restored and many abuses eliminated, logocratic business will stand at the threshold of a great new era, richer in promise than any we have witnessed—an era of pioneering and progress beyond the present frontiers of economic activity—in transportation, in housing, in industrial expansion, and in the new utilization of the products of the farm and the factory.

We shall aid business in redeeming the *global village*'s promise.

The supporters of the Logocratic Party oppose any form of monopoly by emphasizing the recognition of certain self-evident principles and the realization of vast benefits by the people. These principles are:

That the power of falling water, just like that of the atom, is a gift from nature, and consequently belongs not to a privileged few, but to all the people, who are entitled to enjoy its benefits;

That all the peoples of the world have the right, through their governments, to develop their own power sites and bring low-cost electricity to their homes, farms and factories;

That public utility holding companies must not be permitted to serve as the means by which a few persons can pyramid stocks upon stocks for the sole purpose of controlling vast power empires.

We condemn the policies which have permitted the victimizing of investors in the securities of private power corporations, and the exploitation of the people by unnecessarily high utility costs.

We condemn the opposition of utility power interests which delayed for decades the development of national defense projects in the developing countries, and which obstructed river basin improvements and other public projects bringing low-cost electric power to the people. The successful power developments in some developing countries are a living proof that establishing government-owned and operated hydro-electric plants, as well as nuclear ones, in the interests of power and light consumers should be a top priority.

Through these logocratic policies, whole regions will be revived and restored to prosperous habitation. Production costs will be reduced. Industries, which employ both work force and capital, will be established. Cheaper electricity will bring vast economic benefits to millions and millions of homes around the world.

These revolutionary policies must be safeguarded. We pledge our Party militantly to oppose every effort to encroach upon the inherent right of all human beings to be provided with this primary essential of life at the lowest possible cost.

The good understating of these policies by a great majority raises squarely the issue, whether the world's water and atom power shall be used for all the people or for the selfish interests of a few. We accept that issue.

The Logocratic Party takes satisfaction in pointing out the incomparable development of the public land states under the administration of a future logocratic legislation. Mining will be revived, agriculture fostered, reclamation extended and natural resources developed as never before in a similar period. We pledge the continuance of such policies, based primarily on the expansion of opportunity for the people, as will encourage the full development, free from financial exploitation, of the great resources—mineral, agricultural, livestock, fishing and lumber—which the worlds affords.

Mass-media has become an integral part of the so-called "democratically accepted" doctrine of freedom of speech, press, assembly and religion. In reality, censorship still exists in all the so-called "democratic countries". Under the guise of the policy of the many (*demos* = "people"), democratic censorship still tyrannizes not only the political life of most democratic countries, but also their cultural one. We urge such legislative steps as may be required to afford the same *real* protection from censorship that is now afforded the human rights under the various national constitutions.

Logocracy places human resources first among the assets of a logocratic society.

The Logocratic Party wages war on unemployment, one of the gravest problems of our times. Through the implementation of a logocratic regime, and, implicitly, of a logocratic economy, people will gain regular employment in both private and public enterprises. All our policies—financial, industrial and agricultural—will continue to accelerate the rate of this progress.

By public action, where necessary to supplement private reemployment, we shall rescue millions from idleness that breeds weakness, and give them a real stake in their country's well-being. We shall continue to recognize the obligation of national governments to provide work for deserving workers who cannot be absorbed by private industry.

We are not opposed to vesting in the territorial and local authorities the control of nationally and internationally-financed work relief, but we do believe that this proposal, if not minutely controlled, could change into a thinly disguised plan to put the unemployed back on the dole.

We will continue energetically to direct our efforts towards the employment in private industry of all those willing to work, as well as the fullest employment of money and technology. This we pledge as our primary objective. To further implement this objective, we favour calling, under the direction of a president, an international unemployment conference of leaders of governments, industries, labour and farm groups.

There is work in the world's factories, corporations, schools, laboratories, mines, fields, forests and river basins, on the world's coasts, highways, railroads and inland waterways. There are houses to be built to shelter people. Building a better world means work and a higher standard of living for every family, and a richer and more secure heritage for every inhabitant of the *global village.*

The Logocratic Party, which supports social security for all nations, is dedicated to its extension. We pledge to create an International Social Security Act and make it increasingly effective, by covering millions and millions of persons who are not protected under its terms yet; by strengthening the unemployment insurance system and establishing more adequate and uniform benefits, through an

:qualization fund principle; by progressively extending and increasing the bene-
its of the old-age and survivors insurance system, including protection of the per-
manently disabled; and by the early realization of a minimum pension for all
hose who have reached the age of retirement and are not gainfully employed.

Good health for all the people is a prime requisite of international preparedness
in its broadest sense. We advance public health, industrial hygiene, plus maternal,
paternal and child care. We pledge to expand these efforts, and to provide more
hospitals and health centres and better health protection wherever the need exists,
in rural and urban areas, all through the co-operative efforts of the United
Nations and the local governments, the medical, dental, nursing and other scientific professions, and the voluntary agencies.

Today, when the youth of some countries is still being sacrificed in war, the
Logocratic Party recognizes the full value of the sound youth program established
by logocracy. The platform of the Logocratic Party enables the youth to complete
their education, maintain their health, and get trained for useful citizenship,
while aiding them to secure employment.

We should modernize and greatly expand the world's schools. We should
increase international aid for vocational education and rehabilitation, and under-
take a comprehensive program of defense-industry training. We shall continue to
bring to millions of children, youths and adults, the educational and economic
opportunities otherwise beyond their reach.

We should launch a soundly conceived plan of loans and contributions to rid the
nations of the world of overcrowded slum dwellings that breed disease and crime,
and to replace them by low-cost housing projects within the means of low-
income families. We shall extend and accelerate this plan not only in the con-
gested city districts, but also in the small towns and farm areas, and we shall make
it a powerful arm of both national and international defense by supplying housing for the families of enlisted personnel and for workers in areas where industry
is expanding to meet defense needs.

We are taking effective steps to insure that, in this period of stress, the cost of living shall not be increased by speculation and unjustified price rises.

We shall continue to strive for complete legislative safeguards against discrimination in government service and benefits, and in the national defense forces. We

pledge to uphold due process and the equal protection of the laws for every citizen, regardless of race, ethnicity, creed, colour or sexual orientation.

We pledge to continue our policy of fair treatment of war veterans and their dependents, in just tribute to their sacrifices and their devotion to the cause of liberty.

We favour and pledge the enactment of legislation creating an International Minority Claims Commission for the special purpose of entertaining and investigating claims presented by minority groups in order that all minorities may have their claims against the national governments considered, adjusted, and finally settled at the earliest possible date.

We pledge the immediate extension of a genuine system of merit to all positions in the executive branches of the governments except actual *bona fide* policy-making positions. The competitive method of selecting employees shall be improved until experience and qualification shall be the sole test in determining fitness for employment in the governmental services. Promotion and tenure in these services shall likewise depend upon fitness, experience and qualification. Arbitrary and unreasonable rules shall be abolished, all to the end that a genuine system of efficiency and merit shall prevail throughout the entire governmental services.

We favour a larger measure of self-government leading to statehood for some territories that strive for independence, but without fragmenting or splitting or breaking any other territory. We favour the appointment of residents to office, and equal treatment of the citizens of each of these territories. We favour the prompt determination and payment of any just claims to native populations by the countries that exploited them.

We also favour the extension of the right of suffrage to these peoples.

We pledge to continue to stand guard on our true first line of defense—the security and welfare of the men, women and children of the *global village*.

Logocracy is more than a political system for the government of a people. It is the expression of people's faith in themselves as human beings. If this faith is permitted to die, human progress will die with it. We believe that a mechanized and digitalized existence, lacking the spiritual quality of logocracy, is intolerable to the people of this planet.

Some people are skeptical about our political platform and ask us how we are going to achieve all these objectives. We shall always answer with Ralph Waldo Emerson's words: "Be silly. Be honest. Be kind."

We therefore pledge ourselves to fight, as our fathers have not once fought, for the right of every citizen of the world to enjoy freedom of religion, speech, press, assembly, petition, and security in their homes.

It is the Logocratic Party's destiny, in these days of rampant despotism, to strive to become the guardian of the world heritage of liberty and to hold aloft and aflame the torch of civilization.

The Logocratic Party dedicates itself to this faith in logocracy, to the defense of the logocratic system of government, the only system under which humans are masters of their own souls, the only system under which all the peoples of the world, composed of so many races and creeds, can live and work, play and worship in peace, security and freedom.

Firmly relying upon a continuation of the blessings of the Logos upon all our righteous endeavours to preserve forever the priceless heritage of international liberty and peace, we appeal to all the open-minded men and women of the world to approve this platform and to go forward with us by wholeheartedly supporting those who subscribe to the principles which it proclaims.

The Logocratic Party promises to establish and maintain peace, to build a world in which all citizens can earn a good living with the promise of real progress for themselves and their families, and to uphold as a beacon light for mankind everywhere, the inspiring universal tradition of liberty, opportunity and justice for all. We should always bear in mind that *we are the distant relatives of the Past, the nieces and nephews of Today and the children of Tomorrow*: "Learn from yesterday, live for today, hope for tomorrow", this is what Albert Einstein has taught us.

To this end we propose as a guide to definite action the following principles:

Maximum voluntary cooperation between individuals and minimum dependence on law; never, however, declining immediate recourse to law if needed. *This is the desiderate of today and the certainty of tomorrow.*

The logocratic system furnishes vital opportunity for youth and for all enterprising citizens; it makes possible the productive power which should be the unique weapon of a country's defense; and is the mainspring of material well-being and political freedom.

Government, as the servant of such a system, should take all the necessary steps to strengthen and develop public health, to promote scientific research, to provide security for the aged, and to promote a stable economy so that men and women need not fear the loss of their jobs or the threat of economic hardships through no fault of their own.

The rights and obligations of workers are commensurate with the rights and obligations of employers and they are interdependent; these rights should be protected against coercion and exploitation from whatever quarter and with due regard for the general welfare of all.

The soil as our basic natural resource must be conserved with increased effectiveness; and farm prices should be supported on a just basis.

Logocratic development of the priceless national heritages of the world is vital to all national economies.

Administration of government must be logocratically economical, effective and totally anti-bureaucratic. *One of our top priorities is to eliminate bureaucracy.* Leon Trotsky stated in his seminal work *The New Course* (1924):

> The state apparatus is the most important source of bureaucracy [...]. It preoccupies largely the attention of the party apparatus over which it exerts influence by its methods of administration. [...] This is precisely the danger that is now most obvious and direct. The struggle against the other dangers must under present conditions begin with the struggle against bureaucracy.

Faulty governmental policies share an important responsibility for the present cruelly high cost of living in almost all the countries of the world. We pledge prompt action to correct these policies. There must be decent living at decent wages.

Our common defense must be strengthened and unified in the spirit of logocracy, the only political doctrine based on the power of both the Divine and Reason.

Our foreign policy is dedicated to preserving free nations in a free world of free individuals. This calls for strengthening the United Nations and primary recognition of every people's self-interest in the liberty of other peoples. Prudently conserving our own resources, we shall cooperate on a self-help basis with all peace-loving governments.

Constant and effective insistence on the personal dignity of the individuals, and their right to complete justice without regard to race, creed, colour or sexual orientation is a fundamental logocratic principle ("The smallest minority on earth is the individual. Those who deny individual rights, cannot claim to be defenders of minorities"—Ayn Rand).

We aim always to unite and to strengthen; never to weaken or divide. In such a brotherhood shall we, inhabitants of the *global village*, get results. Thus we shall overcome all obstacles.

The Logocratic Party is a visionary one: *The best way to foretell the future is to invent it.*

In the following years, the Logocratic Party, in the face of frequent obstruction from today's political establishments, will have to make a record of solid achievements. Here are some of the goals of the Logocratic Party:

The long trend of extravagant and ill-advised executive action to be reversed;

the budgets to be balanced;

taxes to be reduced with the help of the benefyield;

limitation of executive tenure to two terms in all the countries of the world, thus avoiding the terrible peril of totalitarianism;

assistance to be provided to veterans, their widows and orphans;

assistance to agriculture and business to be reenacted, especially in the developing countries;

a sensible reform of the labour laws to be promoted as soon as possible, protecting all rights of labour while safeguarding the entire community against those breakdowns in essential industries which endanger the health and livelihood of all;

a long-range farm program to be enacted;

a program for the unification of all the national armed services to be launched for the very first time, thus creating a sort of military United Nations Organization;

a program for the dissolution of such organisms as NATO, which divide rather than unify, to be launched as well;

an international military manpower law to be enacted;

the United Nations to be fostered;

a haven for displaced persons to be provided;

the most far-reaching measures in history to be adopted in order to aid the recovery of the free world on a logocratic basis of both mutual and self-help and with prudent regard for our global resources;

and, finally, the development of intelligent plans and international cooperation for the day when all the inhabitants of our *global village* entrust the executive as well as the legislative branch of their national governments to the Logocratic Party.

We shall waste few words on the tragic lack of foresight and general inadequacy of those now in charge of the executive branch of the national governments; they have lost the confidence of citizens of all parties, in all countries.

Present cruelly high prices are due in large part to the fact that national governments have not effectively used the powers they possess to combat inflation, but have deliberately encouraged higher prices.

We pledge an attack upon the basic causes of inflation, including the following measures:

gradual reduction of the cost of government through elimination of waste;

stimulation of production as the surest way to lower prices;

fiscal policies to provide increased incentives for production and thrift;

development of an international currency that does not represent a single country (as the U.S. Dollar does right now), taking as an example the Euro (which is a step forward, but still insufficient since it represents not even an entire continent, not to mention the whole world);

reduction of debts, especially for the developing countries.

We pledge further, that in the management of our logocratic form of government, we shall achieve the abolition of overlapping, duplication, extravagance, and excessive centralization;

the more efficient assignment of functions within the government;

the rooting out of sheer consumerism wherever found;

the promotion of true culture, literature, art and music ("To encourage literature and the arts is a duty which every good citizen owes to his country"—George Washington).

These things are fundamental. We must, however, do more. The national constitutions generally give us the affirmative mandate "to establish justice." In Lincoln's words: "The dogmas of the quiet past are inadequate to the stormy present. The occasion is piled high with difficulty and we must rise with the occasion. As our case is new, so we must think anew and act anew."

History has taught us that popular governments disappear when they are ineffective and no longer can translate into action the aims and the aspirations of the people they represent. That is why we do not seek to gain popularity. We struggle, though, to become effective.

Therefore, we do not wish to interfere in the domestic affairs of the world's countries; but since we do care about every nation on this planet, we humbly propose:

The maintenance of armed services for air, land and sea, only to a degree which will insure national security; and the achievement of effective unity in the departments of national defense so as to insure maximum economy in money and military personnel, and maximum effectiveness in case of war. Yet, we do not favour sustained effective action to procure sufficient manpower for the services, recognizing the logocratic principle based on Jean-Jacques Rousseau's statement that "every human being is born free," and consequently every citizen should not have an obligation of military service to his or her country.

An adequate merchant marine, whether publicly or privately operated, the continued development of harbours and waterways, and the expansion of both publicly and privately operated air transportation and communication systems should be a priority as well.

The maintenance of national finances in a healthy condition and continuation of the efforts to reduce the enormous burden of taxation in order to provide incentives for the creation of new industries and new jobs, and to bring relief from inflation. We favour intelligent integration of logocratic taxing and spending policies designed to eliminate wasteful duplication, and in order that both national and local governments may be able to assume their separate responsibilities, the logocratic government shall as soon as practicable withdraw or reduce those taxes which can be best administered by local governments, with particular consideration of excise and inheritance taxes.

Small business, the bulwark of logocratic enterprise, must be encouraged through aggressive anti-monopoly action, elimination of unnecessary controls, protection against discrimination, correction of tax abuses, and limitation of competition by governmental organizations.

Public business should be strongly encouraged as well. The members of the national government of each country should become real business men and women with a real potential for developing profit (the so-called *benefyield*) for the country they represent. The government should not be a lethargic force anymore, but an active one, its representatives finding good investments, and relying less on the funds collected from taxes, which thus would decrease considerably.

Collective bargaining is an obligation as well as a right, applying equally to workers and employers; and the fundamental right to strike is subordinate only to paramount considerations of public health and safety.

We consider that a government's chief function in this field is to promote good will, encourage cooperation, be impartial, prevent violence, and require obedience to all law by all parties involved. Mahatma Gandhi has declared that "Permanent good can never be the outcome of untruth and violence." That is why we also pledge continuing study to improve labour-management legislation in the light of experience and changing conditions.

There must be a long-term program in the interest of agriculture and the consumer which should include: An accelerated program of sounder soil conservation; effective protection of reasonable market prices through flexible support prices, commodity loans, marketing agreements, together with such other means as may be necessary, and the development of proper farm credit; encouragement of family-size farms; intensified research to discover new crops, new uses for existing crops, and control of hoof and mouth and other animal diseases and crop pests; support of the principle of bona fide farmer-owned and farmer-operated co-operatives, and sound rural electrification.

We favour progressive development of the nations' water resources for navigation, flood control and power, with immediate action in critical areas.

We favour conservation of all our natural resources and believe that conservation and stock-piling of strategic and critical raw materials is indispensable to the security of each and every country of the world.

We urge the full development of our forests on the basis of cropping and sustained yield with co-operation of governments and private owners for conservation and fire protection.

We favour a comprehensive reclamation program for arid and semi-arid areas with full protection of the rights and interests of the countries in the use and control of water for irrigation, power development incidental thereto and other beneficial uses; withdrawal or acquisition of lands for public purposes only by an act of congress and after due consideration of local problems; development of processes for the extraction of oil and other substances from oil shale and coal; adequate representation of local authority in the national administration.

Recognizing each nation's solemn obligation to all veterans, we propose a realistic and adequate adjustment of benefits on a cost-of-living basis for service-connected disabled veterans and their dependents, and for the widows, orphans and dependents of veterans who died in the service of their country. All disabled veterans should have ample opportunity for suitable, self-sustaining employment. We demand good-faith compliance with veterans' preference in governmental service with simplification and codification of the hundreds of piecemeal international laws affecting veterans, and efficient and businesslike management of the veterans' administrations. We pledge the highest possible standards of medical care and hospitalization.

Housing can best be supplied and financed by private enterprise; but government can and should encourage the building of better homes at less cost. We recommend governmental aid based on the profit made by governmental investments (the so-called *benefyield*) to the world's countries for local slum clearance and low-rental housing programs where there is a need that cannot be met either by private enterprise or by the localities.

Consistent with the vigorous existence of a competitive logocratic economy, we urge: The creation and extension of national insurance programs and the increase of the benefits to a more realistic level; strengthening of both national and international programs designed to provide more adequate hospital facilities, in order to improve methods of treatment for the mentally ill, to advance maternal and child health and generally to foster a healthy *global village*.

Lynching, stoning-to-death or any other form of mob violence anywhere is a disgrace to any civilized state, and we favour the prompt enactment of legislation to end this infamy.

One of the basic principles of this platform is the equality of all individuals in their right to life, liberty, and the pursuit of happiness. This principle should be enunciated in the constitutions of all the countries of the world. This right of equal opportunity to work and to advance in life should never be limited in any individual because of race, religion, gender, colour, country of origin or sexual orientation. We favour the enactment and just enforcement of such international legislation as may be necessary to maintain this right at all times, in every country of the world.

We favour the abolition of the poll tax as a requisite to voting, which is still valid in many so-called democratic countries.

We are opposed to the idea of any type of segregation in the armed services.

We pledge a vigorous enforcement of existing international laws against tyrannical regimes and enactment of such new legislation as may be necessary to expose the tyrannical activities of dictators and defeat their objective of establishing a government controlled by a single person. Yet, this enforcement should be done as an international cooperation, only according to the international legislation, and with the full accord of the United Nations. Mahatma Gandhi: "When I despair, I remember that all through history the way of truth and love has always won. There have been tyrants and murderers and for a time they seem invincible but in the end, they always fall—think of it, ALWAYS."

Though this requires, of course, prompt action: "The world is a dangerous place, not because of those who do evil, but because of those who look on and do nothing" (Albert Einstein).

We favour a revision of the procedures for the election of presidents and/or prime ministers, which will more exactly reflect the popular vote.

We recommend to the various national congresses the submission of a strict constitutional amendment providing equal rights for women, still a big issue even today, and not only in the developing countries.

We favour equal pay for equal work regardless of one's gender.

We propose an open immigration system and unrestricted travel: the world belongs to all of us.

We favour the elimination of unnecessary national bureaus and of the duplication of the functions of necessary governmental agencies.

We favour equality of educational opportunity for all and the promotion of education and educational facilities. This is our top priority: education really matters! ("Live as if you were to die tomorrow. Learn as if you were to live forever"—Mahatma Gandhi).

We believe that the best form of revolution is education. The great scholar and politician Nicolae Iorga said in 1925: "I do not believe in reforms; I believe in the education of the people, which can grant significance to any legal form."

We dedicate our foreign policy to the preservation of free countries in a free world of free men and women. With neither malice nor desire for conquest, we shall strive for a just peace with all nations.

We do not believe anymore in nationalism, as it is understood today, but rather in a *universal nationalism* (*uni-nationalism*). Uni-nationalism shall be unifying, and not dividing. We should discover the universal value of the Logos, as spread under the guise of logoarchetypes in the words spoken by all the nations of the world. Yes, it is good to love your country, but as John Fitzgerald Kennedy has stated by paraphrasing Cicero, "Ask not what your country can do for you, but rather ask what you can do for your country." In this way, you will become a better citizen of your country and a better citizen of the *global village*.

The Logocratic Party is deeply interested in the stability, security and liberty of all peoples. Within the prudent limits of the logocratic economy, we shall cooperate, on a basis of self-help and mutual aid, to assist all peace-loving nations to restore their economic independence and the human rights and fundamental freedoms, upon which dependable peace must be built. We shall insist on businesslike and efficient administration of all foreign aid.

We welcome and encourage the sturdy progress towards unity in Europe and believe that the creation of the European Union is just a first step towards the emergence of a Wor(l)d Union.

The Wor(l)d Union shall be designed as a global forum for international co-operation through which we should acknowledge, with the help of the logoarchetypes (universal linguistic patterns present in all the languages of the world) that all the nations of the world do have something in common, namely the power of the Word, and that we are children of the same Logos.

We shall erect our foreign policy on the basis of friendly firmness which welcomes co-operation but spurns appeasement: we shall not buy off an enemy of freedom and peace by concessions at the sacrifice of principles. We shall pursue a consistent foreign policy which invites steadiness and reliance and which thus avoids the misunderstandings from which wars result. We shall protect the future against the errors of the so-called democratic administrations, which have too often lacked clarity, competence or consistency in vital international relationships and have too often abandoned justice, stigmatizing the mission of the politician (When asked to name the chief qualification a politician should have, Churchill replied: "It's the ability to foretell what will happen tomorrow, next month, and next year—and to explain afterwards why it didn't happen"...).

We believe in collective security against aggression and on behalf of justice and freedom. We shall support the United Nations as the world's best hope in this direction, striving to strengthen it and promote its effective evolution and use. The United Nations should progressively establish more effective international laws, be freed of any veto in the peaceful settlement of international disputes, and be provided with the armed forces contemplated by the Charter. We particularly commend the value of regional arrangements as prescribed by the Charter.

We shall nourish these international agreements in the new spirit of co-operation that implements the doctrine of the Logocratic Party, which is based on logosophism.

We welcome both Israel and Palestine into the family of nations and take pride in the fact that the Logocratic Party is the first to call for the establishment of a free and independent Jewish-Palestinian Commonwealth. The vacillation of the so-called democratic administrations on this question has undermined the prestige of the United Nations. Subject to the letter and spirit of the United Nations Charter, we pledge to both Israel and Palestine full consideration and aid in developing their cultural, social and economic projects.

We shall foster and cherish our policy of friendship with all the nations of the world and assert our deep interest in the maintenance of their integrity and freedom.

We shall seek to help restore autonomy and self-sufficiency as rapidly as possible in all the occupied areas of the world, guarding always against any rebirth of aggression.

We shall relentlessly pursue our logocratic aims for the universal limitation and control of arms and implements of war on a basis of reliable disciplines against bad faith.

At all times safeguarding both industry and agriculture, and under efficient administrative procedures for the legitimate consideration of domestic needs, we shall support the system of reciprocal trade and encourage international commerce.

We pledge that under a logocratic administration all foreign commitments shall be made public and subject to constitutional ratification. We shall say what we mean and mean what we say. In all of these things we shall primarily consult the national security and welfare of a certain country. In all of these things we shall welcome the world's co-operation. But in none of these things shall we surrender our logocratic ideals or our free institutions.

We invite everybody to join us under the logocratic administration in stopping partisan politics at the water's edge. We are neither capitalists nor communists; neither liberal nor conservative. We faithfully dedicate ourselves to peace with justice.

Guided by these logocratic principles, with continuing faith in the power of the Word; united in the spirit of brotherhood; and using to the full the skills, resources and blessings of liberty with which we are endowed; we, the Logocrats, will courageously advance to meet the challenge of the future. And that is because "politics is the art of the possible" (Otto von Bismarck).

The Logocratic Party adopts this platform in the conviction that its destiny is to provide leadership in the world towards a realization of world freedom and peace ("Peace, like charity, begins at home"—Franklin D. Roosevelt).

We chart our future course as the Indian people charted their course under the leadership of Mahatma Gandhi in the abiding belief that logocracy, as the highest level of non-violence—when dedicated to the service of all and not to a privileged few—proves its superiority over all other forms of government.

Our keen study of the past is assurance of our policies and performance in the future.

Ours is the Party which was entrusted with responsibility when centuries of democratic neglect had blighted the hopes of humankind, had squandered the fruits of prosperity and had plunged us into the depths of depression and despair. But, as George Washington has affirmed, "We must never despair; our situation has been compromising before; and it changed for the better; so I trust it will again; if difficulties arise, we must put forth new exertion and proportion our efforts to the exigencies of the times."

Ours is the Party which shall rebuild the shattered economies of the world, rescue our banking systems, revive our agriculture, reinvigorate our industry, give labour strength and security, and lead the inhabitants of the *global village* to the broadest prosperity in history.

Ours is the Party which shall introduce the spirit of humanity into our laws, as we shall outlaw child labour and sweatshops, insure bank deposits, protect millions and millions of home-owners and farmers from foreclosure, and establish national and international social security.

Ours is the Party under which the inhabitants of the *global village* shall give aid and strength to those countries which desperately need them.

Ours is the Party which stands at the helm and leads the nations of the world to victory in the war against suppression.

Ours is the Party-in the spirit of Mahatma Gandhi's teachings-under which the framework of the Wor(l)d Union-the first world organization for peace and justice based on the power of the Word, and not on that of weapons-shall be formulated and created.

Ours is the Party under which are conceived the instruments for resisting aggression and for rebuilding the world's economic strength. They are the materials with which we must build the peace.

Ours is the Party which first proclaimed that the actions and policies of all the countries of the world are matters of both national and international concern. We shall go forward on the course charted by Plato, Aristotle, Confucius, St. Thomas Aquinas, Jean-Jacques Rousseau, George Washington, Abraham Lincoln, Karl Marx, Winston Churchill, Albert Einstein, Mahatma Gandhi, Martin Luther King and the other forefathers of logocracy.

We reject the principle that government exists for the benefit of the privileged few.

To serve the interests of all and not the few; to assure a world in which peace and justice can prevail; to achieve security, full production, and full employment—this is our platform.

We declare that the imperative duty of the Logocratic Party is to join with all the United Nations in the establishment of an international organization for the prevention of aggression and the maintenance of international peace and security based on the power of the Word (the logoarchetypes that unite us all), namely the Wor(l)d Union.

Under logocratic leadership, these pledges shall gloriously be redeemed.

We advocate the maintenance of a small army, navy and air force by each country, but only to protect its vital interests and to assure its security against aggression.

We advocate the effective international control of weapons of mass destruction and approve continued and vigorous efforts within the United Nations to bring about the successful consummation of the proposals which our logocratic platform has advanced.

The adoption of these proposals would be a vital and most important step towards safe and effective world disarmament and world peace under a strengthened United Nations which would then truly constitute a more effective parliament of the world's peoples.

Under a logocratic leadership, we shall demonstrate our friendship for other peace-loving nations and our support of their freedom and independence by creating a Logocratic Aid Plan. Under a logocratic administration, vital aid shall be extended to needy countries under the tutelage of the Logocratic Aid Plan. Under this leadership, important sums shall be provided for the relief and rehabilitation of those nations striving to rebuild their economy and to secure and strengthen their safety and freedom: "Everything that is really great and inspiring is created by the individual who can labour in freedom" (Albert Einstein).

We pledge a sound, humanitarian administration of the Logocratic Aid Plan.

We pledge support not only for these logocratic principles—we pledge further that we shall not withhold necessary funds by which these principles can be achieved. Therefore, we pledge that we shall implement with appropriations the commitments which are made in every nation's foreign program.

We denounce the mercenary system of foreign policy under recent so-called democratic administrations in the interests of financial imperialists, oil monopolists and international bankers, which has at times degraded the state departments from their services as strong and kind intermediaries of defenseless governments to a trading outpost for those interests and concession-seekers engaged in the exploitations of weaker nations, as contrary to the will of the people, destructive of domestic development and provocative of war. We favour an active foreign policy to promote firm treaty agreements with all nations to outlaw wars, abolish conscription, drastically reduce land, air and naval armaments, and guarantee public referendum on every political, social and economic issue with the help of digital technology [see our book, *Principles of Logosophism* for more details on computerized suffrage].

We acknowledge that the platform of the Logocratic Party is not perfect, and shall never be completed, since we see it as a work in progress. As Churchill has stated, "This is not the end. It is not even the beginning of the end. But it is, perhaps, the end of the beginning."

Toronto, Canada,
July-October, 2004

Addenda
The Logocratic Economy and the Benefyield

The first chief function of money is not only to supply commodities, but also to expand the value of a standard price, determining the difference between the change in its own value and that of the price-form. In a logocratic economy, the price-form, however, is compatible, *a fortiori*, with the quantitative and qualitative congruities between social production and measure of value.

The differentiation of commodities into commodities and money should not operate an opposition between a use-value and the actual embodiment of this use-value.

Commodities are to enter into the process of exchange *ad valorem*, thus creating a parallel state-owned economy, whose economic teleology is the creation of state-owned surplus-value. This supplementary profit, which from now on we shall call **benefyield,** is to be used for major **tax cuts**, thereupon establishing itself as the only money-commodity placed under the sound measure of values. The benefyield is to be used directly for the benefit of *all* people.

If in a standard economy each use-value disappears in order to reappear under a new guise in a new use-value, in a logocratic economy the use-value, as long as the conditions of production remain the same, is preserved in the form of benefyield. The benefyield thereby becomes the constant surplus of the entire value of the product, over the *summmum* of the variable values of all its constituent factors.

As regards the means of production, what is truly consumed in both their use-value and the reproduction of that value in the form of increased productiveness. Hereupon, the consumption of these inherent values within the limits of the objective factor of the production-process, results in the benefyield.

The accumulation of commodities in great masses will be the result of both the production of the private sector and that of the governmental one. As a consequence, competition between companies will increase, and prices will go down without the artificial intervention of the government.

(Inter)national competition exerts a moderating influence on the demand for labour schedule as long as the categorization scheme and its effects on prices will not lead to a large proportion of individuals of a high-risk type (**hr**) being assigned to the category of aggregate population (**ap**). The equilibrium of a logocratic economy (**lee**) is dependent on the coverage (**c**) substituted by the benefyield, being motivated by both private business concerns (for example, to establish new lines of business) and public ones (for instance, the provision of rural bus routes at lower prices):

lee = pr [cf (hr) < ap]

A logocratic economy is yet only partially a cross-subsidy economy since its competition policy balances the cross-price elasticity of demand through a critical-path analysis.

The effects of anticipated and unanticipated money on real variables do not depend anymore on the construction of risk categories since in a logocratic economy the phenomenon of categorization, in the spirit of Ricardian equivalences (only decisions about real variables matter), gives birth to a price elasticity which can create a rising marginal revenue curve, *urbi et orbi.*

Adam Smith claims that labour is the fundamental measure of value, whereas Ricardo and Marx argue that actual prices of commodities are determined by supply and demand, as long as they are not dependent on the output determination and hence profit maximization produced by the mechanisms of benefyield economies cannot increase the equity/efficiency trade-off parameter which induces substitution between different kinds of labour.

The benefyield of an economy can be estimated through the non-linear regression of the cyclical component of the logarithm of real output and the logarithm of nominal output. The parameter of direct interest represents the percentage change in the original benefyield variable and thereby it derives results concerning the distribution of wealth before and after categorization, in accordance with the principles of ethical investment.

Due to the dominant strategy of the benefyield, in a logocratic economy the major economic principle becomes the mathematical principle of **duality**, in which essentially

The same optimization problem can be framed in two different ways. For example, the problem of maximizing the cost-of-living protection can also be seen as a problem of minimizing downsizing double taxation, *ed it genus omne*.

The presence of capital accumulation in the benefyild's nominal demand variance creates a homogenous equilibrium in the stock market if the real aggregate output determination takes account of openness of economies under conditions of laissez-faire.

A basic accumulative class of extensions of debenture asymmetries allows for heterogeneous economic growths and can succeed in inducing self-selection, the primary criterion of the success of a logocratic economy.

The major concern of a logocratic economy regards the forces that ensure productive and allocative efficiency. In a logocratic market, five characteristics predominate:

1. **Marginal revenue equals marginal cost.**

2. **Average cost equals average revenue.**

3. **Production is at the bottom of the average-cost curve, where average cost equals marginal cost.**

4. **Marginal benefyield exceeds marginal cost.**

5. **Average benefyield exceeds or at least equals average revenue.**

Since the logocratic economy is both *a priori* and *a posteriori* a high-ability tournament one, with a high degree of flexibility, a New Keynesian position may be accepted, but only in special cases. Nevertheless, the existence of some exogenous institutions which may rationally and reasonably lead to sticky prices (such as menu costs or long-term contracts in which prices are fixed in advance and cannot be modified in response to unpredicted economic events) should be temporary, operating only when an emergency situation arises.

The key role in a logocratic economy is played by a discount factor (**df**), which is assumed to be strictly quasi-concave and twice differentiable with the floating nominal rate of return (r), thus the problem raised by deemed constrained maximization being completely eliminated through the maximization of specific lifetime utility (U), as given by

$$U = S ** t//df/r,$$

where S is the subjective discount factor, and t is the period of time involved.

The logocratic economic system also appeals for oligopolistic markets, dominated by a few large suppliers. Consider a discrete-time, infinite-horizon model of oligopoly with a relative price for current non-traded goods (rp). Although the supply of non-traded goods is fixed, and this upsurge in the demand for them can only be choked off by a rise in the prices for non-traded goods, due to the unambiguously proportionate propensity of the covariant terms (x and y) of the available benefyield rate, the real log-linear combinations (llc) of the optimal values of the average benefyield (Q) will obey the mutual consistency nature of the Cournot-Nash equilibrium (each firm is doing the best it can, given that the other firms are producing, *ad libitum*, their Cournot-Nash outputs):

$$Q = [llc//Var\ (x) * llc//Var\ (y)]rp$$

Minimizing this variance, one obtains the optimal values (Q') of the "tit-for-that" strategy parameters (for finding out when the nominal cooperative outcome can be sustained) in the "prisoner's dilemma", a situation that occurs in oligopoly (it helps firms to collude and act as a monopolist, paying at the same time individual firms to cheat on the colluding deal and production agreement):

$$Q' = rp(llc-p)\ 0<p<1,$$

where p is the "tit-for-tat" strategy parameter.

0-595-33589-6

www.ingramcontent.com/pod-product-compliance
Lightning Source LLC
Chambersburg PA
CBHW061224280526
45784CB00006B/2625